942.8   Martell, Hazel Mary
MAR   The Vikings and Jorvik

DATE DUE			

HIDDEN WORLDS

THE VIKINGS and JORVIK

by Hazel Mary Martell

DILLON PRESS
New York

First American publication 1993 by Dillon Press, Macmillan Publishing Company, 866 Third Avenue, New York, NY 10022

Macmillan Publishing Company is part of the Maxwell Communication Group of Companies.

First published in Great Britain by Zoë Books Limited

A ZOË BOOK

Devised and produced by
Zoë Books Limited
15 Worthy Lane
Winchester
Hampshire SO23 7AB
England

Printed in Italy by Grafedit SpA
Design: Jan Sterling, Sterling Associates
Picture research: Suzanne Williams
Illustrations: Shane Marsh, Cecilia Fitzsimons
Maps: Gecko Limited
Production: Grahame Griffiths

10 9 8 7 6 5 4 3 2 1

Library of Congress Cataloging-in-Publication Data

Martell, Hazel.
    The Vikings and Jorvik / Hazel Mary Martell.
        p. cm — (Hidden worlds)
    Includes index.
    Summary: Describes how relics and artifacts found in York, England, provide clues to the everyday life of Vikings who established a settlement there called Jorvik in the ninth century.
    ISBN 0-87518-541-X
    1. York (England) — Antiquities — Juvenile literature. 2. Vikings — England — York — History — Juvenile literature. [1. Vikings — Social life and customs. 2. York (England) — Antiquities. 3. Excavations (Archaeological) — England — York. 4. Archaeology.] I. Title. II. Series.
DA690.Y6M37 1993
942.8'4301— dc20   92-25215

Photographic acknowledgments
The publishers wish to acknowledge, with thanks, the following photographic sources:

British Museum: 8t; David Collison 27b; Copenhagen University, Denmark: title page and 8b; Robert Harding Picture Library 7b / Philip Craven, 26; University Museum of National Antiquities, Oslo: kitchen utensils from the Oseberg find 24t; Antikvarisk-topografiska arkivet, Stockholm: 24b, 27t, 29b; Woodmansterne Picture Library: 6 / Jeremy Marks; York Archaeological Trust Picture Library: front cover, 7t, 9, 10, 11t & b, 12t & b, 13, 14, 17t & b, 20t & b, 21, 22, 23t & b, 29t & b; Zefa: 5.

Contents

Introduction

The Vikings were a group of people who lived more than 1,000 years ago in the countries we now call Norway, Denmark, and Sweden. They are first mentioned in a book called the ***Anglo-Saxon Chronicle***. It tells us that three Viking ships arrived on the south coast of Britain in A.D. 789. The Vikings are next mentioned in A.D. 793, when they raided the **monastery** at Lindisfarne, also called Holy Island, on the coast of Northumberland. They stole all the monastery's treasures, killed some of the **monks**, and took others away to be sold as slaves.

There were many more Viking raids on the coasts of Britain and Europe. Many monasteries were raided because the Vikings knew that they were often full of treasures and were not guarded by soldiers. Since the only people who could read and write at this time were monks and priests,

▼ The Viking Age lasted from the end of the 8th century to the late 11th century. This map shows the world that the Vikings knew. Unlike most other people at that time, the Vikings dared to sail out of sight of land. The name "Viking" means "to go across the seas."

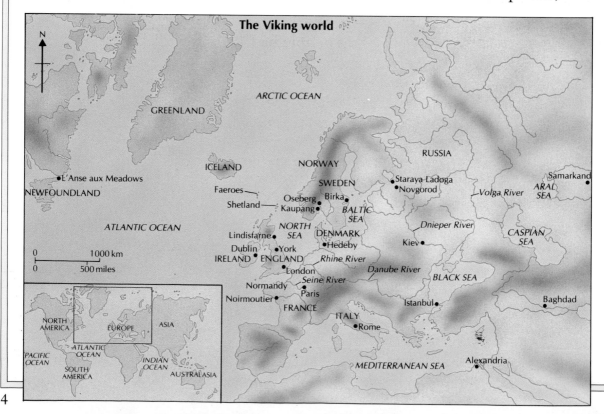

The Viking world

ARCTIC OCEAN

GREENLAND

RUSSIA

ICELAND

NORWAY

•L'Anse aux Meadows

Samarkand

NEWFOUNDLAND

Faeroes

SWEDEN

•Staraya Ladoga
•Novgorod

ARAL
SEA

Shetland

Oseberg• Birka•
Kaupang•

Volga River

BALTIC
SEA

ATLANTIC OCEAN

NORTH
SEA

Dnieper River

CASPIAN
SEA

Lindisfarne•

DENMARK

Dublin• •York
IRELAND • ENGLAND

•Hedeby

Kiev•

0   1000 km

Rhine River

0   500 miles

•London
Seine River

Danube River

BLACK SEA

Normandy

•Paris

Noirmoutier•

FRANCE

ITALY

Istanbul•

Baghdad

•Rome

NORTH
AMERICA

EUROPE

ASIA

PACIFIC
OCEAN

ATLANTIC
OCEAN

INDIAN
OCEAN

MEDITERRANEAN SEA

Alexandria
•

SOUTH
AMERICA

AUSTRALASIA

The Vikings were successful because they were such good shipbuilders. Their ships were strong, and they were constructed so that they did not break up in rough seas. They could either be rowed or sailed on seas or on rivers. They could also land on beaches in places where there were no harbors. Some Vikings were buried in their ships when they died. This ship is part of a burial that was excavated at Gokstad in Norway.

▼ One reason why the Vikings left their homelands was that there was not enough good farmland for everybody. As you can see from this photograph, Norway is mountainous, with only narrow strips of fertile land alongside the fjords. Much of Sweden was either boggy or thickly wooded, and Denmark had large areas of sandy heath land.

they wrote about the Viking raids and violence. They did not write about any good things the Vikings might have done.

For many centuries, the monks' work provided the only knowledge that people had of the Vikings. More recently, however, **archaeologists** have begun to build a different picture of these people. Although the Vikings were sometimes warlike and violent, they were also excellent shipbuilders and metalworkers, as well as being farmers. As traders and settlers, they sailed from their homes to Britain, Ireland, France, Russia, Iceland, Greenland, and North America. Some Vikings went to Byzantium (now called Istanbul), where they met up with traders from eastern places such as Baghdad and China. In A.D. 867, Vikings captured the English town of Eoforwic (now called York) and made it into a great trading center which they called Jorvik. Jorvik remained an important Viking center until the **Norman Conquest** in 1066.

The history of Jorvik

The place the Vikings called Jorvik was originally known to the British as Caer Ebrauc. Little is known about it until the year A.D. 71, however, when the Roman Ninth Legion marched there from Lincoln to put down a rebellion. The rebels were the local people, known as Brigantes, and they were protesting against Roman rule. To try to keep the peace in the area, the Romans first built a wooden and then a stone fortress between the Ouse and Foss rivers. They called it Eboracum. A civilian settlement grew up around it. By A.D. 306, when the Roman emperor Constantine visited Eboracum, the town had become an international trading center.

One hundred years later, the Roman legions left Britain and the first groups of Angles, Jutes,

▼ Not all of York's history is buried. Although the wall that surrounds the city today is mainly medieval, parts of it are Roman. The most substantial part is the Multangular Tower, shown here. It was added to the fortress walls soon after A.D. 300. The stonework at the top is a medieval addition.

and Saxons arrived from across the North Sea. They settled in and around Eboracum, which they called Eoforwic. By 600, Britain had been divided up into several small kingdoms. One of these was **Northumbria**, and in 627 its king, Edwin, was converted to Christianity in Eoforwic. It became a center of Christianity and of learning. One of its scholars, Alcuin, wrote about the Viking raid on Lindisfarne in A.D. 793.

In 867 Eoforwic was attacked and defeated by the Vikings. They changed the town's name to Jorvik, and by 876 some of the Vikings had started to settle as farmers in the countryside surrounding the town. Others settled as craftworkers and **merchants**, and by 919 Jorvik had the first of its Viking kings. The last of them was killed in 954, but the Vikings remained important in Jorvik for another 100 years.

In 1068 William the Conqueror and his army of Norman invaders reached Jorvik and built a timber castle there. Early the following year, the people rebelled and attacked it. William returned and built a second castle, but that was also attacked with the help of an army commanded by the sons of the king of Denmark. This second rebellion was firmly put down, and Jorvik's links with the world of the Vikings were gradually broken.

▲ This helmet was found on Jorvik's Coppergate site by two construction workers. It is Anglo-Saxon, not Viking, and dates from around A.D. 750.

◄ Clifford's Tower was built in the 13th century on the site of one of William the Conqueror's two castles in York. It is very close to Coppergate.

Why choose this site?

▶ A coin from the reign of Erik Bloodaxe, who was king in Jorvik from A.D. 947 to 948 and again from 952 to 954.

▲ *Egill's Saga* tells the story of Egill Skallagrimsson and his family in Norway, Iceland, and England. This picture of him was painted in the 17th century to illustrate a collection of Icelandic sagas. These stories were passed on by word of mouth and were not written down until the 13th century.

Archaeologists knew from written records such as old books and stories that the Vikings had been in York during the 9th, 10th, and 11th centuries. The *Anglo-Saxon Chronicle* tells of a Viking army coming to the eastern kingdom of Britain, **East Anglia**, and staying through the winter of A.D. 866. In the following year, the *Chronicle* says, the army captured York. Three years later, the Vikings had taken nearly all of England. The area they lived in was called the **Danelaw**. Only the part known as **Wessex** remained free. Its king, **Alfred**, defeated the Vikings in 878 and then started to win the rest of the country back from them. By the time of his death in 899, he had almost succeeded. Only Northumbria, with its capital at Jorvik, remained strongly Viking. The *Chronicle* records that by 919, Jorvik had a Viking king named Ragnald.

Other Viking kings followed Ragnald, until in 954 the last king was killed at the Battle of Stainmore. He was Erik Bloodaxe, the son of Harald Fairhair, the first king of Norway. We know a lot about Erik Bloodaxe from *Egill's Saga*, which is one of the oldest Viking stories, or **sagas**. In the saga, Egill tells about his visit to Jorvik and about seeing Erik Bloodaxe in his palace there.

Egill also tells about trade between Jorvik and Iceland, where he lived for most of his life.

Archaeologists had other evidence for the Vikings in York, too. Over the years, various things made by the Vikings, their **artifacts**, had been found in the city. Then in 1972, the York Archaeological Trust had the chance to dig out, or **excavate**, the cellars of a building in a street known as Pavement. There they found more Viking Age artifacts, including boots and shoes and iron knives with wooden handles and leather sheathes to put them in.

This glimpse into the Viking Age made the archaeologists want to discover more. However, finding a site for a large excavation in a city is difficult. Usually, all the land is built over and there are no open spaces. In York the archaeologists were lucky. A site became available in 1976, some 200 feet away from the earlier excavation.

▼ Combs like these have been found at sites throughout the Viking world. We know that the Vikings were proud of their appearance. One Englishman complained that Vikings attracted all the women because they washed and combed their hair so much!

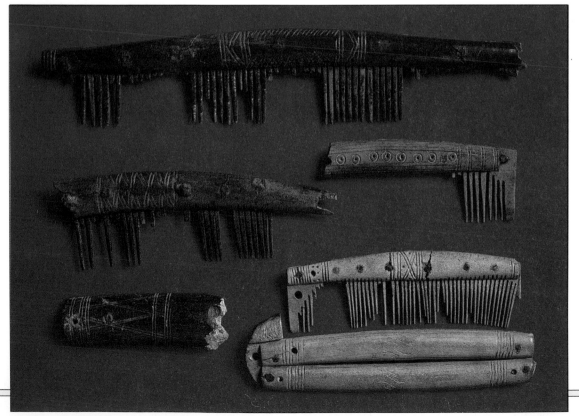

Excavation and recording

▶ An aerial view of the Coppergate site when the excavation, or dig, was in progress. Coppergate is the street that runs between the excavation and the church. The bottom of the picture shows how the ground sloped down toward the Foss River in Viking times. In winter the site was roofed over to protect the dig and the diggers from the worst of the weather.

The site that the archaeologists were able to excavate was in a street called Coppergate. This name may well be of Viking origin, as it is made up of two Old Norse words. All the Vikings spoke some form of this language. *Copper* is probably a variation of the Old Norse word *koppari*, which means "cupmaker," and *gate* is from the Old Norse word *gata*, which means "street." This makes it possible that Coppergate was the street of the cupmakers in Viking times.

Working on the site

The archaeological team started work with heavy drills and sledgehammers. These were used to remove the bases, or **foundations**, of some fairly modern buildings. After that, digging was done more carefully. The team removed 34,000 different levels or **layers** of soil and debris that had built up over the Viking Age remains. All the layers revealed something about the people who had lived in that part of York through the centuries. However, the layers from the Viking Age were of the greatest interest.

Archaeologists used trowels and hand shovels and even fine brushes to remove the soil from the most delicate objects. As they excavated, each layer was numbered and recorded. All the objects they found were washed on the site and labeled with the number of the layer in which they were found. They were then put in bags and boxes to be examined later by **specialists**.

The team then took many photographs to make a record of the site. They also took measurements and made drawings of areas that would not show well on photographs.

▲ Archaeologists spend a lot of time measuring and drawing, as well as digging up and recording artifacts.

◀ Some of the walls on the Coppergate site were over 3 feet high. They are the best-preserved Viking Age buildings discovered in Britain so far. Because the Coppergate site is very damp, no air could reach the timbers to rot them once they had been buried by soil and debris. The archaeologists found enough evidence at the site to be able to make reconstructions of the Viking buildings. These are now inside the Jorvik Viking Center.

▲ The first picture shows a metal padlock as it was found at the Coppergate dig. It was covered in rust. The padlock could not be cleaned or conserved in any way until it had been X-rayed to find out if there was any solid metal left.

The second picture shows what the X ray revealed. The light-colored areas are the rust, but underneath them the pattern on the metal can be clearly seen.

Analysis and conservation

The soil in the Coppergate area is very damp. It preserved many of the Viking Age artifacts that would have rotted away at a drier site. As well as the timbers for the houses and workshops, archaeologists found objects made of leather, cloth, pottery, bone, antler, metal, and wood. Although the artifacts had survived in the waterlogged soil, the condition of many of them would soon change if they were exposed to the air. They would begin to shrink as they dried out, then crack, and eventually they would fall apart. To prevent this from happening, a person called a **conservator** worked on the site. The conservator made sure that all the finds were packed correctly for their journey to the laboratories. There the objects were examined, or analyzed, to see what they were made of. They were then treated, or conserved, so that they would stay in good condition.

In the laboratories

Once the artifacts reached the laboratories, they were analyzed to see how they were made. Their condition was also checked so that the archaeologists could decide on the best way to conserve them. Many objects of bone, stone, and glass were simply washed clean. Other materials needed more complex treatment. For example, the wooden objects were placed in a bath of special wax. Some fragile objects were painted with a hard glaze or **resin** to make them stronger. Rusted metal objects had to be **X-rayed** to find the solid metal beneath the layers of crumbling rust, or **corrosion**, before any work could be done on them.

In the laboratories tests were carried out to

decide the age of some of the objects. One of these tests is called tree-ring dating, or **dendrochronology**. First the archaeologists studied the pattern of growth rings on an excavated timber. Then they compared it with the pattern from timber whose age is known. As all trees grow thicker rings in some years than in others, all trees that were growing at a certain time have a similar pattern. By finding a pattern that matches that on their timber, archaeologists could tell when the excavated timber was cut down.

The age of some objects can also be found by a test called **radiocarbon dating**. This measures the amount of **carbon 14** in an object made from wood or any other material that was once alive. All living matter absorbs a certain amount of carbon in its life. Some of this is carbon 14, which is radioactive. Scientists know exactly how long it takes for carbon 14 to decay. By measuring how much carbon 14 is left in an object, they can tell the age of that object.

◀ Sometimes broken objects are restored so that they can be put on display. The original pieces are stuck together, and any missing bits are replaced by modern materials. Careful records are kept of all this work so that everyone knows which pieces are original and which pieces have been added.

Environmental archaeology

Artifacts are not the only things that tell us about life in the past. Seeds, **pollen** grains, bones, and insect remains in the soil can also tell us about the conditions people lived in, the food they ate, and even the diseases they suffered from. The people who study these objects are known as environmental archaeologists.

▲ An environmental archaeologist at work in the laboratory. After the seeds, bones, and other remains have been separated from the soil, they are examined under a microscope and identified.

The environment of Jorvik
In Viking times the city was surrounded by thick forests of oak and ash trees, with hazels and alders growing in between. The archaeologists also know that bread was made from wheat or barley, which was grown in fields where the forest had been cleared.

Health and disease
Viking Jorvik was not a very hygienic place by any standards. The Vikings had no garbage collectors, so garbage was either dumped in pits behind the houses or left to rot in the unpaved streets. Here it was picked over by hens, as well as by mice, black rats, dung beetles, bluebottles, and even ravens and buzzards. The bones of frogs have been found almost everywhere, including inside the houses.

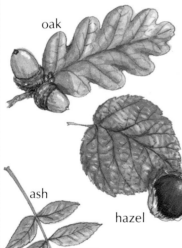

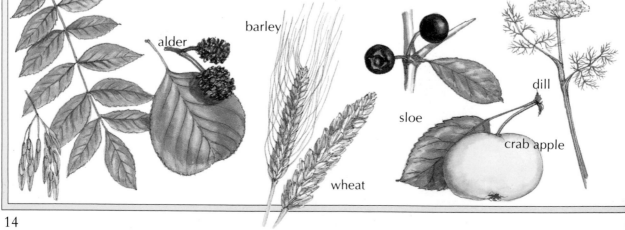

oak

ash

hazel

alder

barley

wheat

sloe

dill

crab apple

Many people kept a pig or two in their backyard, usually next to the well and the lavatory, or **cesspit**. The cesspit was a hole dug in the ground, surrounded by a screen made of pieces of wood. From remains found in some of the lavatories, environmental archaeologists have been able to find out about the Vikings' diet. They have identified the seeds of crab apples and sloes, as well as herbs such as coriander and dill. They also know that many of the Vikings suffered from worms and other **parasites**, including fleas and nits!

▼ Some of the many different plants, animals, birds, and insects that were found in and around Jorvik.

raven

roe deer

cow

sheep

buzzard

pig

chicken

hare

fly

dung beetle

black rat

mouse

flea

louse

nit

tapeworm

frog

At home in Jorvik

The houses in Jorvik stood close together.
They had wooden walls and **thatched roofs**.
The houses were one story high and each had
one room, with an earth floor and an open
hearth in the middle. The hearth was surrounded
by stones to stop the fire from spreading. The
smoke from the fire was supposed to go out
through a hole in the roof. Some smoke stayed
inside the house, however, making it dusty and
dark. Some houses had windows cut into the
walls to let the light in. They also let drafts in,

as there was no glass. At night and in cold weather, the windows were covered with wooden shutters.

Everyday life

The hearth was the center of the Viking home. The people who lived there cooked, slept, ate, spun, wove, and played around it. There was very little furniture. At night, light came from the log fire and from small lamps filled with burning oil. This light was not very bright, so it was often difficult to find anything that fell on the floor. Many small objects, such as brooches and coins, were trampled into the earth and lost. Digging up these objects has helped archaeologists to show us what life was like in Jorvik.

The remains of bones, seeds, and nuts show that the Vikings had a varied diet. They ate apples, plums, raspberries, hazelnuts, and walnuts. Their vegetables included carrots, parsnips, and celery. They also ate oysters, cod, and herring, as well as beef, mutton, pork, goat, and chicken.

▲ This large jar was found in the excavation of Jorvik. It was used for storing food. From its design, archaeologists know that it came from Torksey in Lincolnshire. Food was also stored in big wooden barrels that were held together with iron hoops.

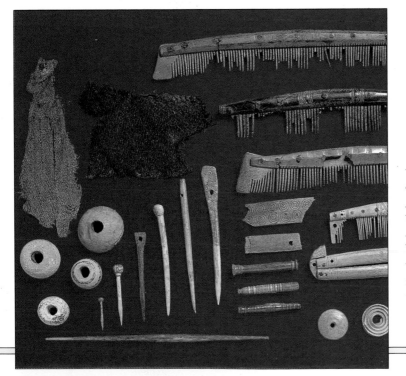

◄ These are some of the artifacts that were found in Jorvik. The combs are made from deer antlers and the pins are made from animal bones. The disklike objects are weights that were used in spinning wool into yarn. The yarn was then woven into cloth like the small piece shown here.

Coppergate reconstructed

By day Coppergate was a busy street. Children played around the houses. Cats, dogs, hens, and geese ran freely, scavenged for food, or slept in the sun. Some people bought household goods, shoes, or jewelry at the stalls the traders set up in front of their houses. Others just stopped to gossip. Sometimes a small cart passed, carrying goods to or from the **quayside**. Laundry was hung outside the houses to dry in the breeze.

The air of Jorvik was full of strong smells. The stink of rotting rubbish mingled with that of cesspits, woodsmoke, **tanning** leather, and manure from the various animals. By the quayside there was probably a strong smell of fish from the barrels of herring that were unloaded there, and flies buzzed all the time.

The scene was a colorful one, however, as the Vikings were fond of bright clothing. Archaeologists know this from analyzing small scraps of cloth found at the site and discovering their original colors. They know that the Vikings made dyes from plants such as madder, woad, and weld. These were used to make the colors red, blue, and yellow, and two or more dyes could be used together to make different colors. Both men and women wore jewelry to hold their clothing in place and also to show how wealthy they were.

▼ An artist's reconstruction of a scene in Coppergate during the Viking Age. If you look carefully at the man in the bottom right-hand corner, you will see that he is wearing a pendant around his neck. This represents Thor's hammer and was worn by many Vikings as a kind of good luck charm. Thor was the most popular of the Viking gods. He was said to have red hair and a laugh that rumbled like thunder. He was not very smart and often had to use his hammer as a weapon to get himself out of trouble. The most important of the Viking gods was Odin, but he was not as popular as Thor.

Craftwork

▶ Viking shoes and boots were made of leather. They had a flat sole that was made in one piece and sewn on to the upper part of the shoe. When the sole wore through, it was taken off and a new one was sewn in its place. Both shoes and boots were made to be slipped on and off the foot, but boots were held in place with a leather thong that fastened around the ankle.

Many people who lived in Jorvik earned a living by making things to sell, both in the city and farther afield. Some people worked in their houses, but most of them built special workshops on the narrow plots of land behind their homes. Like the houses, the workshops had earth floors. By excavating some of these, archaeologists have found out not only what sorts of objects were made but also how they were manufactured. From this evidence, they know that the craftworkers in Jorvik included woodworkers, metalworkers, leatherworkers, and jewelers.

▶ A woodworker made these cups from a piece of solid wood. They were cut to roughly the right shape and then fixed into a machine called a pole-lathe. By pressing down the treadle with his foot, the woodworker made the piece of wood spin on the lathe. As the wood spun around, the woodworker held a chisel or gouge against it and shaped the cup inside and out.

Potters made pots for cooking or for storing food such as flour and grain or liquids, but cups and plates were made from wood. So, too, were barrels and chests for storing clothes and valuable possessions. The woodworkers probably also made some furniture, but very little evidence of this has survived.

The metalworkers made knives and spoons, locks and keys, hinges, pans, chains, hooks, nails, and tools for themselves and other craftworkers. Some metalworkers also made jewelry, such as brooches and cloak pins, from silver, gold, bronze, and lead. A very few metalworkers were also allowed to make, or **mint**, coins.

The leatherworkers made shoes and boots, sheaths for knives, belts, and fastenings. The leather came from the skin of cattle that were butchered in the city.

Cattle and other animals also provided the bones that were made into simple objects such as ice skates, knife handles, **spindle whorls**, dice and playing pieces. The boneworkers also cut and carved deer antlers to make combs and decorated strap ends that prevented wool belts from fraying.

▼ There were glassmakers in Jorvik, but they could only make small quantities of glass at a time. Some of the glass was colored and was used to make beads like these.

0   1cm

0      $^1/_2$ in.

Merchants and traders

There were no stores in Jorvik. Instead, the craftworkers sold their goods from stalls or **booths** set up in the street in front of their houses. Farmers from the villages around the city probably brought in various sorts of food to sell in the market, so the people of Jorvik would be well supplied with everyday things.

Many craftworkers also had money to spare for luxuries. These included goods such as wine, furs, and a patterned silk called **brocade**, and jewelry made from **amber**, ivory, **jet**, and silver. None of the raw materials for these goods were produced in Jorvik. They were all brought by merchants and traders from other parts of Britain or from overseas.

The simplest way these people made a living was to buy goods made by one person and then sell them to someone else at a profit. The other way was known as **bartering**. This involved exchanging one set of goods for another of equal or greater value.

Archaeological evidence for this trade in Jorvik includes pieces of silk, pottery, fine jewelry, millstones for grinding grain into flour,

▶ Amber and jet were two of the raw materials that traders brought to Jorvik. They sold the roughly cut pieces to the jewelers, who then made them into rings, necklaces, and pendants. Most of this jewelry was sold in Jorvik, but sometimes it was sold to people called chapmen. The chapmen took a selection of small items to sell to farmers who lived in the remote countryside.

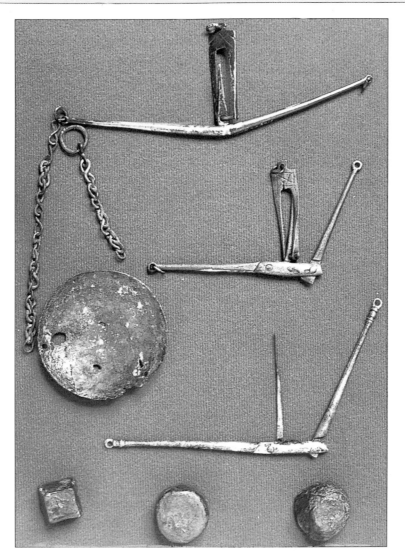

◀ The early Viking traders did not use coins in buying and selling goods. Instead, they used pieces of silver, which they cut up and weighed on portable scales. The silver was often called hack silver. It was put in one pan and balanced with lead weights in the other pan.

▼ The Vikings who settled in Britain began to use silver coins. These were made by stamping a piece of silver sheet between two iron **dies**, which were engraved with the pattern, or type, for the two sides of the coin.

   Archaeologists found two of these iron dies at Coppergate. One was broken, but the other was complete and was dated to A.D. 920. Dies were tested on a strip of lead to make sure that they had been made correctly. The strip of lead in this picture is from the reign of King Eadwig, who ruled England from 955 to 959. The die for one side of the coin was correct, but the die for the other side had been engraved the wrong way, so it could not be used!

honestones for sharpening the blades of knives and other tools, and **soapstone** bowls, which were used as cooking pots.

   Other luxury items such as furs, whale oil for lamps, unusual foods, and spices have disappeared without a trace, but we know from written evidence that Viking traders in Jorvik imported them. We also know from the sagas that the traders exported grain, honey, and wool from Jorvik to Iceland.

On the quayside

Jorvik was a busy port. Although the town was a long way inland, ships could be sailed or rowed up to its center from the North Sea, using the Humber River and then the Ouse River, which flowed through the city. The Foss River also flowed through Jorvik and joined the Ouse to the east of Coppergate. There were wooden **wharves**, quays, and warehouses on the banks of both these rivers, and ships from all parts of the Viking world might be found alongside them at any time.

While some people were unloading the ships, others would be busy mending the sails and ropes or repairing any damage that had occurred on the voyage. In the Viking Age, most shipbuilders constructed the framework first, and then the planks

▲ A merchant ship with a crew of six or seven men and a cargo of four or five tons could travel the 1,500 miles between Jorvik and North Norway in about two weeks. Food and drink for the voyage was stored in wooden barrels and tubs like these, which were found in the Oseberg ship burial in Norway.

▶ This carved stone from Gotland in Sweden shows a Viking ship in full sail. As ropes and cloth soon rot away in the ground, archaeologists have to rely on pictures like this to tell them what the sails looked like and how they were used. However, no one is sure whether the diamond shapes on the sail are ropes for moving it about or a pattern in different colored cloth.

24

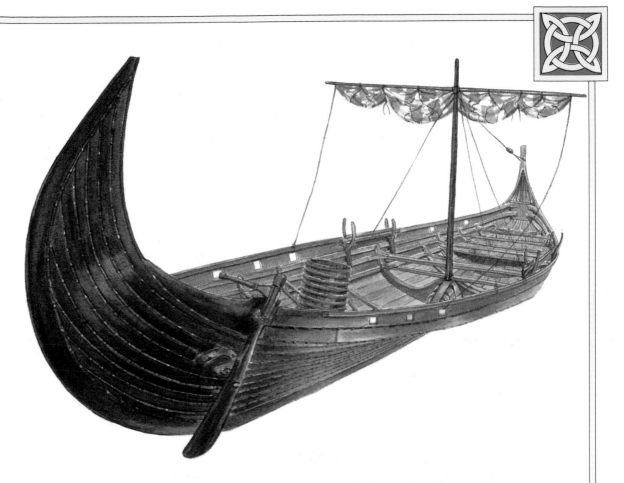

were nailed on to it. This made them rigid, which meant they often broke up in rough seas. In a Viking ship the planks were nailed together before the framework was added. This kept them flexible, so they did not break up, even in stormy seas.

Many different types of speech, or accents, would be heard, although all the Vikings spoke Old Norse. This language was very similar to the Old English spoken by the Anglo-Saxons in Jorvik, so they would all be able to understand each other. At a time when only a few people knew how to write, talking was the main way of passing on news, gossip, and messages.

No remains of Viking ships have been excavated in Jorvik yet, but there is evidence from Norway, Denmark, and Sweden to show us what these ships were like and how they were made.

▲ Viking raiders were famous for their longships, which carried a crew of about 60 men and could be rowed at high speeds. The merchants, however, used smaller ships called *knarrs*. Like the longships, they were made from wood, but they were shorter and broader in the middle. They were usually sailed rather than rowed. This one has been reconstructed from evidence found at Skuldelev on the Roskilde Fjord in Denmark.

Jorvik's place in the Viking world

▶ Although most Vikings were farmers, very little evidence of their farmhouses remains. Most of the farms were on land that is still used for farming, so the houses have been rebuilt many times since the Viking Age. The farmhouse at Stong in Iceland, however, was abandoned in A.D. 1104, after a volcanic eruption covered the fields with ash. It was excavated in 1939 and this reconstruction was built, using evidence from the excavation.

Many Vikings turned to trading as a way of making extra money, as there was not enough good farmland to support everyone in their homelands. The traders usually set out in the early summer, when the hay had been gathered and the weather was fine. They then returned home in the early autumn, in time to help with the grain harvest.

Vikings from different areas went trading in different countries. For example, the Vikings from Sweden usually sailed across the Baltic Sea and then made their way along the Russian rivers to the Black Sea and Byzantium. Along the way they established trading posts at Staraya Ladoga, Novgorod, and Kiev. The Vikings from Norway went to Iceland, the Scottish islands, the Isle of Man, and Ireland, where they set up trading centers in places such as Dublin and Waterford. Danish Vikings came to the east coast of England, trading with people who lived in the Danelaw. The Vikings who came to Jorvik, however,

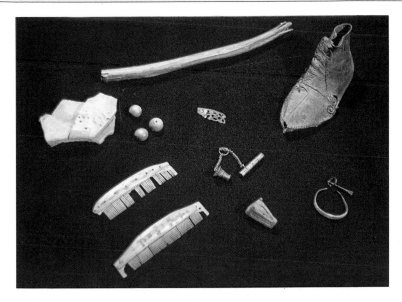

◄ In Russia, archaeologists have found evidence of goods exported by the Vikings. These items are from Staraya Ladoga and similar artifacts have been found in Kiev, Novgorod, and Smolensk.

▼ Before the Vikings became Christians, they buried their belongings with them when they died. This collection of pottery and glassware was excavated from some merchants' graves in the Viking market town of Birka in Sweden. These goods were imported from the Rhineland and central Europe.

were probably a mixture of Danes, Norwegians, and Icelanders. They traded with the Swedish Vikings, as well as with the Anglo-Saxons, the Scots, and the Irish. This ensured that Jorvik would be known throughout the Viking world and that ships from many different places would trade there.

Trade links

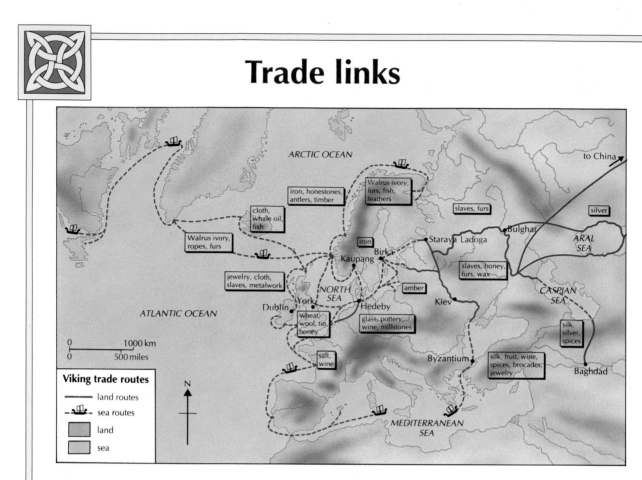

Labels on map:
- ARCTIC OCEAN
- to China
- iron, honestones, antlers, timber
- Walrus ivory, furs, fish, feathers
- slaves, furs
- silver
- cloth, whale oil, fish
- Bulghar
- ARAL SEA
- Walrus ivory, ropes, furs
- iron
- Staraya Ladoga
- Birka
- Kaupang
- slaves, honey, furs, wax
- CASPIAN SEA
- jewelry, cloth, slaves, metalwork
- NORTH SEA
- amber
- ATLANTIC OCEAN
- Dublin
- York
- Hedeby
- Klev
- silk, silver, spices
- wheat, wool, tin, honey
- glass, pottery, wine, millstones
- Byzantium
- silk, fruit, wine, spices, brocades, jewelry
- Baghdad
- salt, wine
- MEDITERRANEAN SEA

- 0 1000 km
- 0 500 miles

Viking trade routes
- ——— land routes
- ⊶⊶ sea routes
- land
- sea

N

▲ This map shows the main trading routes used by the Vikings and the goods they transported. There were important Viking trading centers at Kaupang in Norway, Birka in Sweden, Hedeby in Denmark, Dublin in Ireland, as well as Jorvik.

Archaeologists have found plenty of evidence to show that Jorvik had trading links with other parts of Britain and the rest of the Viking world. For example, some types of stone are found only in certain places. The stone for the small honestones that people carried on their belts came from Norway, as did much of the soapstone for the cooking pots. In contrast, the volcanic **lava** that made the best millstones for grinding came from the Rhineland in Germany.

Wine also came from the Rhineland, while whalebone, whale oil, and walrus-hide ropes were brought from Iceland and the far north. Iceland provided dried and smoked fish, too, and special pins and brooches came from Scotland and Ireland. Silk was made only in China and in parts of the Islamic and Byzantine empires, yet several pieces of it have been found in Jorvik. The silk

28

was probably bought in Byzantium, but the Vikings are also known to have traveled farther east.

Coins from Jorvik have been found in Denmark. There were also close trading and political links between Jorvik and Dublin, since both centers were ruled by the same Viking king in the 10th century. Goods from Jorvik probably also went to the Viking homelands, as British artifacts have been found in all the major trading centers from this period.

The Vikings traded in luxury goods. Their ships were designed to carry small loads quickly, and so they were well suited to this trade. By the middle of the 11th century, however, trade in Europe had changed. Bulky goods took the place of luxury goods and bigger ships were needed. The Viking traders lost their importance in Jorvik and elsewhere. The Viking Age came to an end and evidence of its existence was slowly buried by the debris left by the people who followed.

▲ Archaeologists can learn a lot about trade links from the coins they find. This coin was found at Coppergate. Its Arabic inscription tells archaeologists that it was minted for Ishma'il Ibn Achmad, who was caliph of Samarkand in the early part of the 10th century. Samarkand was over 3,000 miles from Jorvik, and the coin, which was a forgery, probably came by way of Scandinavia, where many thousands of Arab coins have been found.

◀ Many Vikings had their favorite possessions buried with them when they died. Archaeologists have excavated some of the graves and found out where the different items came from. This tells them more about the trade links used by the Vikings. All the items in this picture were found in Sweden.

Glossary

Alfred: King of Wessex from A.D. 871 to 899. He defeated the Vikings at the battle of Edington and made them agree to the Treaty of Wedmore. The treaty allowed the Vikings to live in the part of England known as the Danelaw (see below) if they became Christians.

amber: the fossilized resin of pine trees. It is usually dark yellow.

Anglo-Saxon Chronicle: a written record of events in England. It was started in the reign of Alfred but included the history of the country back to A.D. 1.

archaeologist: someone who studies objects from the past in a careful and scientific manner.

artifact: any object made by people.

bartering: using goods instead of money to buy other goods.

booth: a temporary shelter over a market stall.

brocade: a heavy cloth made from silk. It has a raised pattern woven into it.

carbon 14: a radioactive form of carbon that is absorbed by all living creatures.

cesspit: a hole in the ground that is used as a lavatory.

conservator: a person who examines each artifact and then decides how best to preserve it.

corrosion: a process in which an object, such as solid metal, is eaten away by a chemical reaction.

Danelaw: the part of Britain in which the Vikings were allowed to live under their own laws. It included Northumbria, East Anglia, and the Five Boroughs of Lincoln, Stamford, Derby, Nottingham, Leicester, and the Southwest Midlands.

dendrochronology: finding the age of a piece of wood by studying the pattern of its growth rings and comparing them with wood of a known age.

die: a hard metal object carved with a pattern that can be stamped on to softer metal or leather.

East Anglia: one of the ancient kingdoms of England.

excavation: the place where archaeologists dig to find information about the past.

foundation (I): the sturdy structure underneath a building that holds it up.

foundation (II): the start, or establishment, of something.

hearth: a solid area where a fire can burn without spreading.

jet: a black rock that looks like coal but is light and clean. It is used to make jewelry.

lava:	a very hard rock of volcanic origin.
layer:	a thickness of soil or debris that is all of the same age. Some layers are only $\frac{1}{2}$ inch depth and 1 or $1\frac{1}{2}$ inches long.
merchant:	someone who earns a living through buying and selling goods and raw materials.
mint:	to make coins officially, usually with the king's permission.
monastery:	a collection of buildings where religious men or women live and worship.
monks:	men who live in a monastery.
Norman Conquest:	the invasion of England by William the Conqueror, which started in 1066.
Northumbria:	one of the ancient kingdoms of England.
parasites:	animals, plants, and insects that can only live on another living creature.
pollen:	a yellow dust produced by flowers that fertilizes the seeds.
quayside:	a platform alongside a river where ships are loaded and unloaded.
radiocarbon dating:	finding the age of an object by measuring the amount of carbon 14 it contains.
resin:	a substance that can either be obtained from some plants or be made. It can be used to strengthen other materials.
saga:	a story from Viking times. The sagas were originally learned by heart and passed down from one generation to the next. Many were written down in the 13th century by Snorri Sturluson from Iceland.
soapstone:	a soft stone that can be carved easily.
spindle whorl:	a round weight with a hole in the middle. It was put on the bottom of a spindle so that the yarn would spin smoothly.
specialist:	someone who concentrates on one area of knowledge.
tan:	to make skin or hide into leather by soaking it in a substance called tannin.
thatched roof:	a roof made from a thick layer of straw, reeds, or heather.
Wessex:	one of the ancient kingdoms of England. Its capital was at Winchester.
wharf:	a platform or landing stage where ships can be loaded and unloaded.
X ray:	an invisible ray that can be used to take photographs of the inside of some objects through the outer covering.

Index